CW01649931

A HISTORY OF SUNSHINE AND SHADOWS

A HISTORY OF SUNSHINE AND SHADOWS

Elizabeth Haden

The Book Guild Ltd
Sussex, England

This book is sold subject to the condition that it shall not, by way of trade or otherwise, be lent, re-sold, hired out, photocopied or held in any retrieval system or otherwise circulated without the publisher's prior consent in any form of binding or cover other than that in which this is published and without a similar condition including this condition being imposed on the subsequent purchaser.

The Book Guild Ltd.
25 High Street,
Lewes, Sussex

First published 2000
© Elizabeth Haden

Set in Bembo
Typesetting by
SetSystems Ltd, Saffron Walden, Essex

Printed in Great Britain by
Bookcraft (Bath) Ltd, Avon

A catalogue record for this book is available from the British Library

ISBN 1 85776 505 2

Chilly the day long years ago
And many years have passed, not slow.
It was early morning I was born.
Through this time both healed and torn

Let me now recall the road
When I sat in baby clothes Mother had carefully sewed
The pram, the tassels, grass and sun
Watching my siblings in play having fun.

A historic place is Greenwich Park
Wherein is played many a lark
Not only yesterday, but now it seems
And from the hill the river gleams.

New Cross is not so far away
And there we lived our early days.
A rented flat, so dark and dim
And small concrete yard to play in.

Then came the day that Dad would say
The time has come to move away.
Brave was he to work so hard
To give us a garden and not a yard.

A Deptford house was found and sound
Small garden where flowers abound.
Three small children would have a tree
To play in safety and be free.

Money was counted and plans were made
The house was Dad's, the money paid
Possessions packed, the van was stacked.
Could there be anything that we lacked?

Front door was oak, the bricks were red
Through these portals, we were led.
Joy for Mother, and Dad was glad.
A great house, for his girls and lad.

John Evelyn School some steps away
Where we would spend our infant days
Past the corner shop where we would stop
A halfpenny spent on a lollipop.

Then one Friday in fading light
We three with Mother and hands held tight
In gas-lit streets we walked around
To Deptford High Street where shops were found.

Mother searched to stretch a pound
Through stalls lamp-lit with hissing sound
Piled with apples, pears and veg.
Some lamb for Sunday – yes a leg.

Laden then, with money spent
Happy and tired home we went
Past the building round and drab
The Central Hall, we must not lag.

So homeward through dim-lit roads
We finally reach the family abode.
Shopping unpacked and put away
Kettle on stove, no time to play

Wireless tuned to Children's Hour
Not electricity – but acid battery powered.
Tea was laid, a place for each
Dad and Mother by example teach.

Washing up, a task to share
An hour to play without a care.
The zinc bath from the yard came in
Three baths enjoyed in joyous din.

And then to bed we were led
Tired, clean and happy and fed
Little oil lamps lit the room
And morning came all too soon.

We rise again and down the stairs
We find our breakfast and our chairs.
Excitement rises for today
We are going to Central Hall, not far away.

The magic of the darkened hall
Waiting for the Ink Pen Men to enthral
Followed then by Mickey Mouse
Cheers and laughter fill the house.

Home again and Sunday looms
Hymns to be sung all out of tune
At the Little Hall where we were taught
Of Mary, Joseph, Jesus and good thought.

Sunday tea another treat
Shrimps and winkles bought in the street
Jellies and cakes the Sunday bake
All the delights would Mother make.

Then to the parlour we would run
Piano, gramophone and songs to be sung
Apples and oranges and games to play
Then all put away for another day.

Monday morning Mother rises at four
Dad to work, a kiss at the door.
It's washing day, the copper lit
Clothes to be washed, every bit.

Soon the sheets flap on the line.
Children up for school in time
Shoes polished all neat and clean
Off to school our lessons to glean.

Then one sunny July day
A lovely surprise came our way
A little sister, a beauty too
Fair curly hair, and big eyes of blue.

Soon with tiny sister we went
It was the Christening event
At that lovely church, St. Luke's its name
It stands there still, and just the same.

Now we four children grew and grew
Blossoming on Mother's roasts and stews
Dad working hard with long hours to do
As tug captain round coast and river too.

Dad would take us if time to spare
To see Laurel and Hardy and sweets to share
There was Rin Tin Tin and Charlie Chaplin
With hoots of laughter the Palace would ring.

Another happening I remember
A misty night in October or November
We rose from bed at Mother's call
Down to the long and chilly hall.

Mother stood, door opened wide
Lined up her finger as a guide.
A great airship in the sky
We watched it silently gliding by.

Never before had we seen such a sight
But it was back to bed eyes shut tight
This wonder to ponder on all night
For all we'd seen were birds in flight.

And now the nights are longer still
Soon we'll see the guy and catherine wheel
Sparklers in hand are whirled around
Bonfire lit, and fireworks loudly sound.

The days are short and nights are longer
We have some pennies but not to squander
And home-made chains will soon festoon
The hall, the scullery and every room.

Mother makes the flour paste
And long lines of chains are made in haste
But on the floor our sticky mess lay
Then time for bed Mother would say.

We made a visit to Lewisham
Father Christmas was there at Chiesman's
We took a ride on the 47 bus
At the clock tower off we rush.

Inside the store, and in his cave
Father Christmas said, 'You must behave
Then on Christmas night I will come
When all the carols have been sung.'

Mother saved all year through
For the Christmas bird and pudding too
Her precious sixpence week by week
Bought the treats that she would seek.

Christmas Eve at last is here
That he will come we have no fear
Cocoa, and biscuits left for him to eat
And a chance for him to warm his feet.

Come early dawn and we awake
The presents were there, we shiver and shake
We decided then to examine some
The pretty wrappings off they come.

At breakfast time we dash downstairs
And drop our presents in the chair
Excited chatter and breakfast eaten
We race to the front room not to be beaten.

A Christmas tree delights our eyes
Bowls of oranges and apples we spy
Nuts and chocolates spread out there
Touch them – no we do not dare.

We've now enjoyed our Christmas fare
Joyous laughter, and not a care
Mother played the piano, and Dad sang
And children's voices to the rafters rang.

Christmas crackers pulled with a resounding crack
We were then bedecked with paper hats
All games played, on nutshells we trod
Then up the stairs to the land of Nod.

Christmas now is fading fast
And it's back to lessons and school at last
There to learn our tables true
To read and write, and friendships renew.

Spring sunshine brightly fills the sky
And there are Easter eggs to buy
But what is this about a Cross
When Jesus to this world is lost.

We learn of his pain and sacrifice
And of the cock that crowed thrice.
So when we say our prayers at night
We ask his help to put the world aright

Mother taught us to be kind
To help the old, the sick, and blind.
Should we be on a bus or tram
Our seat we gave, lest they should stand.

So in that way a good deed was done
Now we were entitled to our fun
A game of hopscotch or spin our tops
Our pleasures simple but enjoyed a lot.

Now with daylight fading fast
We watch the lamplighter cycle past.
At each lamppost he would stop
Raise the pole and the light would pop.

Gentle beams stream down the street
Casting shadows at our feet.
We must beat the hot pie man
As home to Mum and Dad we ran.

'Pies all hot,' he would call out.
Indoors we imitate his shout.
Now to bed we must retire
No lingering by the stove fire.

Another day of work and play
And the cat's meat man is on his way.
He puts the meat upon a stick.
The cat soon learns a clever trick.

At the front door he would wait
His appetite his treat would sate.
He sat there licking jaws and paws.
He had caught it dropping through the door.

From time to time Dad would say
'Let's go and look at the river today.'
From Deptford to Greenwich we would walk
Of barges, cargoes and ships he'd talk.

He told us tales of far off places
Of wheat in holds, and tea in cases
Loaded on these ships so large
And then transferred on to a barge.

He told us then of their history
And how he towed them from the estuary
In bad weather, rain and gale force winds
The journey to the docks begins.

His hours of work not forty-eight
But ninety-six or more to shift the freight.
So that's why we always had to wait
To see Dad if he came home late.

As our legs begin to tire
We look towards Greenwich church spire.
'Come on,' says Dad, 'we'll catch a tram.'
With a sigh of relief on we cram.

There are lots of other people there
From each the conductor takes a fare
Tickets are punched with his machine
As driver and conductor worked as a team.

The tram speeds off along the line
Over Creek Bridge, it stops from time to time
Then Evelyn Street it rumbles along
People get off, and people get on.

The Mansion House is now in view
We are tired and hungry too
At our stop we all alight
Home for tea and buns tonight.

Mother sent me for some milk one day
She gave me a jug and what to say
Half a pint, and fill it please.
The lady laughed, you're being teased.

The dairy was just two streets away
The milkman came with his churn and ladle each day
The baker too with his basket piled high
Would break a cottage loaf in half for you to buy.

The days went past and we grew fast
And to junior school we went at last
Brother to Clyde Street School for boys
Where football became a constant joy.

Big sister and I to Hughes Fields went
There we learnt what lessons meant
Taught our sums and books were read
Putting information in our heads.

Now we had homework too
Not an easy task to do.
With satchels bulging with our books
From the cloakroom our coats we took.

Out we go and homeward bound
Over unfamiliar ground
Past the Victualling Yard we go
With new found friends we'd got to know.

Down Princes Street we would walk
Of the day's happenings we would talk
The public house, the Globe, in sight
Then Evelyn Street, look left and right.

Now we say goodbye to friends
Following the road as it bends.
Arriving home a hug from Mum
Out to the garden then we run.

At the end of the garden in a shed
Are hens and chicks to be fed
We throw the corn for them to eat
Collect the eggs, and then retreat.

Now we have tomorrow's breakfast
A good reward for that feeding task
And pennies saved for Mother's purse.
A lot of people fared far worse

For there were children without shoes
Winter and summer clothes too
And food for them was very scarce, and worse
For unemployment was a curse.

Bad days they were, but no stealing
And people were honest in their dealing
Front doors and windows were left open
No doors or locks were ever broken.

Pawnshops did a roaring trade
Though not a lot of money made.
The symbol of three gold balls
Was recognised by one and all.

In Deptford High Street we often saw
Men begging, injured in the First World War
Pitiful sights with medals galore
They had given so much, their future, and more.

Not many people could spare a penny
But some would give if they had any
They never looked into their faces
People walked by with quickened paces.

Feelings of guilt, and unable to aid
We glanced elsewhere the memory to fade.
Each family had its sorrows and woes
When money is short, how cold the wind blows.

Neighbours rallied around each other
A helping hand was never a bother
Outgrown clothes passed to the needy
Woolly hats and coats all tweedy.

Holidays of sea and sand
Were never in the yearly plan
Nor a ride in a charabanc
In the garden we got our sun-tan.

We had no reason to be sad
For we had a good Mum and Dad
They fed and clothed us the best they could
A family together we proudly stood.

On Sunday evening in Greenwich Park
Where we examined trees and bark
We found initials and hearts carved there
A gentle message of those who dare.

Then Bank Holidays came along
To Blackheath the crowds would throng.
A donkey ride and coconut shy, prizes won to admire
Ice cream and peanuts enjoyed until we tire.

The evenings now are getting dark
Leaves are falling and trees are stark.
Another winter approaches fast
Another year now in the past

Spring is upon us quickly now
Daffodils in the wind do bow.
We play with our tops and skipping ropes
Our spirits rise and our hopes

We collect our wood and nails too
Design our scooters and barrows anew.
Hammers and pincers out they came
The creativity a glorious game.

Made and tested time and again
Our friends bring theirs seeking fame
For the best and fastest we hope to find
The models were never two of a kind.

Big sister was chosen May Queen of Deptford
But could her costume Mother yet afford?
On a bright and sunny day in May
At Hayes Common she joined the glorious parade.

At school with teachers in command
Minds concentrate to every demand
Taught that we must try our best
To meet the Friday morning test.

Scholarships loomed at the age of eleven
Several prayers are sent to heaven
Our talents then are sorted out
For some of us a joyous shout.

Big sister to Greenwich Central went
On her uniform much money spent
Two of this and three of that
And don't forget the special hat.

A difficult time for Mum and Dad
Although both proud and very glad
Their eldest child had made the grade
The clothes were bought, the money paid.

Now we hear a foreign tongue
In French big sister sings a song
And verbs recited in monotone
Our sister studies quietly alone.

Other lessons to us quite strange
Geometry and algebra are in her range
Speech training she is taught as well
Handwriting and long words to spell.

Brother still in Clyde Street School
Football and cricket were his rule
Secondary in his mind were sums.
Sports and races always won

Bumps, bruises and broken arm
Did not deter, despite the harm
But then it dawned, lessons must be done
There were school prizes to be won.

Dad meanwhile working hard and long
But he often sang a happy song.
He planned a holiday for us all
Where we would hear seagulls call

A modest journey by standards now
In fields we might see a cow
A week was picked, train tickets bought
Holiday abode must now be sought

Whitstable was Dad's choice, in Kent.
From Deptford Station off we went
With heavy cases we had walked
To start the first holiday of which we talked

Up the steps we struggled, slow
Panting and puffing faces aglow
Total enjoyment now to be seen
With a chocolate bar from Nestlé's machine.

The railway lines shine in the sun
Soon the great black engine will come
Black smoke billowing from its funnel
Emerging majestically from the tunnel.

Squealing brakes, the train has stopped.
With bag and baggage on we hopped
Anticipation of things new to see
All of us chatting happily.

On through Greenwich and Woolwich too
Past factories, houses and tunnels travelled through.
Dartford now with trees and fields
And so the enchantment builds and builds.

Through Gravesend now we travel on.
Leaning out windows Mother says is wrong
'You'll get dirt and grit in your eye,'
As smoke and red hot smuts fly by.

Station names we read with speed
Following the train map where it would lead
Soon we must arrive it seemed
To begin the holiday of which we dreamed.

Suddenly we can smell the sea
The first time for sisters, brother and me.
The station now comes into sight
The train stops, and we all alight.

Bag and baggage counted with care
Each of us carrying our allotted share
One last look at the engine now
It stands magnificent with a hissing row.

The engine driver waves his oily rag.
As we pick up the luggage, our legs sag.
Not deterred, behind Dad we file
On every face a happy smile.

Out on the narrow High Street pavement
We searched for the address we'd been sent.
There was the house on the corner end
Mrs Reagan greeted us like a family friend.

She led us all to the sitting room
Provided tea and cakes that afternoon.
A lovely lady gentle and kind
She showed us where our beds to find.

We could not wait now to unpack
We had to see the sea in fact.
Across the road and down an alley
Fast on foot we did not dally.

There it was, the greatest sight
The sea, and seagulls swooping in flight
Their cries, a joy for us to hear
For us the sea held no fear.

Over the pebbled beach we ran
To the water edge, the sea to scan.
On the horizon were several ships
Then back we ran for fish and chips

Every day on the beach we play
We swim in the water but do not stay.
We shiver you see, the sea is cold
And around us quickly our towels we fold.

It did not dismay a little bit
In the sea everyday we'd take a dip.
We watched the fishermen mend their nets
Working quickly before the sun sets.

We took long walks in the sea breeze air
For just a few days we had no care
We searched the quaint old village shops
To buy as presents a variety of rocks.

We all had enjoyed a splendid holiday
Now to pack, and on our way.
We board a train that's homeward bound
Back home again to familiar ground

Our train arrives at New Cross Station.
Dad and Mother call us to attention
Off we go with luggage in hand
A happy little family band.

As we walked the road seemed long
But Dad was quietly singing a song
"Holidays all over, money is all spent
How we loved our holiday down in Kent."

And so we walked and we chattered
We'd soon be home, that's all that mattered.
Our heavy luggage made us tired
But we turned into our road inspired.

Home at last, the kettle on for tea
It was good to be home, but we had seen the sea.
As we drank our refreshing drink
Of things we had seen we could sit and think.

'Let's unpack our things,' said Mother
Then up to bed and under the covers.
Eyelids now become heavy and sleepy
We drift off to sleep, sound and deeply.

The holiday did us so much good
Dad said we'd go again if we could.
Perhaps next year if all went well
We would have another seaside tale to tell.

How fortunate we were, we became aware
As stories of the holiday with friends we share
And then the rock we hand around
Hoping all their teeth are sound.

Back to work for Dad, and school for us
Money to earn, and learning a must.
Whitstable would be visited twice again
With sunshine, winds and drizzling rain.

Whilst these holidays were kept in mind
At home there were other things to enjoy and find.
Greenwich held a Pageant of Kings and Queens
Costumes and jewels conjured marvellous scenes.

We sat on seating high in the sky
History unfolding before the eye.
Henry VIII and his Queens were there
Strutting and posing in floodlit night air.

With these scenes we were enthralled
A help in history lessons when recalled.
At the end we stood and loyally sang
God Save the King on a wobbling stand.

Slowly now we eased our way
As we felt the tall stands wobble and sway.
At last our feet were on the ground
And on our way home, the quickest route found.

Now brother entered Grove Street School
To Greenwich Central I went too.
Learn all you can, Mother would say
In the long run it will pay.

Now Greenwich Central was disciplined and strict
The teachers and headmistress spotted every trick.
Hats on straight, and gym slip pressed
We must always appear neatly dressed

Every Monday morning in the Assembly Hall
We walked across the stage straight and tall.
There sat the headmistress, and teachers grim of face
Examining each pupil for cleanliness and grace.

Nervously we returned to our allotted places
Relieved expressions on our faces.
Hymns were sung, and prayers spoken quietly
Each form then marched in line held tightly.

The line was held till form room reached
No word was uttered, lest the silence breached.
Settled at our desks, two pupils at each
A formidable form mistress began to teach.

Maths, history, geography held our attention
Domestic science, needlework also need a mention.
Speech training was always fun, not like some
French, geometry and algebra, never welcome.

At the end of lessons the bell was rung
Satchels packed with homework to be done
Out of the gates, down King George Street
Our minds on work still to complete.

Down Crooms Hill towards the trams
On the right a stretch of the park ran.
The gentle song of birds we hear
And noisy sounds of trams annoy the ear.

At the church the tram stands at the junction
The driver swings its arm, a necessary function.
Soon upon its wooden seats we sit
Willing to stand if we see anyone unfit.

Some days a nature study is planned
And trees with interest are scanned.
As we walk the lanes of Greenwich Park
This gentle lesson has made its mark.

Then back to school to write our notes
Sketches to be drawn, within our scope.
A test would follow, there was no doubt
A price to pay for a period out.

November days always seemed dreary
Waking in the mornings to something eerie
A swirling fog outside the window.
As we dressed for school, the pace was slow.

Reluctant to go to school such days
We could get lost in many ways.
The return journey was much more fun
When the fog hadn't lifted, and darkness come

We listened to fog-horns from the river
Muffled sounds, and passing vague figures.
Corners turned with measured step
Out of the fog, lampposts suddenly leapt.

Mother awaited us at the door.
The kitchen clock had long passed four
Our meal was waiting on the table
Hot cups of tea to drink when we were able.

As a treat some Friday nights
Chestnuts were cooked to our delight
Each one cut and placed on the kitchen range
And each in turn had its place changed.

There they sizzled and sometimes popped
When cooked. Around the room we hopped
Our fingers felt the burning heat
But soon the nuts were ready to eat.

Tomorrow perhaps the coalman would come.
Mother usually ordered half a ton.
With blackened face, heavy sacks on back
Through the house to the cellar he'd track.

With a thunderous roar he emptied his sacks
Till the cellar with coal was heaped and stacked.
We were so thankful then to know
Warm we'd be, come rain come snow.

With the new year came another sport
And excitement of a different sort.
New Cross Speedway came into being
Dad thought this might be worth seeing.

So when our homework had been completed
We walked to the arena, where we were seated.
With a programme we studied the teams
But would it be exciting as it seemed?

A tape was stretched across the track.
Each rider had a number on his back
Astride a bike in coloured suit
Engines fired into life with a right boot.

The tape shot up and off they went
Black cinders in the air were sent
Blue fumes left floating in the air
Corners were taken with expert flair.

The admiring crowd stood up and cheered
As riders manoeuvred and bikes veered
Each looking for a convenient gap
Battling to be first in the winning lap.

This sport with all its danger and glamour
To meet their heroes the crowds would clamour.
Ron Johnson and Tom Fardon, most famous names
Remembered in the Halls of Fame.

We enjoyed the sport throughout the season.
If our heroes failed, we discussed the reason.
Then one evening on a fateful day
We experienced life in a dreadful way.

Our hero Tom Fardon roared away
At the front we hoped he'd stay.
At the corner a mistake was made
Beside his bike Tom Fardon laid.

A gasp went up throughout the crowd
Then silence, not a word aloud.
We watched him stretchered through the gate
For news of him we had to wait.

Finally the news was bad, and sad
No more would we see the gallant lad.
He had died, and the fun was gone
To follow this sport we felt was wrong.

Our evening now with games were filled
At dominoes we became quite skilled
Jig-saw puzzles, and games of snap
A book by the fire read on the lap.

By gas-light books were spread about
Homework done if the mantle didn't burn out.
Dad had heard that cables were being laid
He spoke of the electric current being made.

To us a mystery, a miracle of light
The click of a switch, and a light so bright.
Street lamps were being converted soon.
If Dad could afford it, what a boon.

Discussions were held, Mother nodded her head
There would be no oil lamps when we went to bed.
Somehow together they made their plans
To afford this luxury, it would be grand.

Pennies saved, and make do and mend.
It could be achieved, as and when.
Then one day, after school, home we came.
Mother smiled, we would not light the gas again.

For light now, we flicked a switch
And trembling fingers had a twitch.
Mother encouraged us all in turn.
With this system, no match to burn.

Now homework was done under this wondrous light
And so much better for everyone's sight.
Mother still cooked by gas and range.
The street lighting a welcome change.

We'd miss the man on his bike with pole
For work he would now play a different role.
So this was progress, yet we missed him
He was gone with the gas lamps that were so dim.

The purse strings were always tight
Nothing was bought and claimed as a right.
Men worked hard at any job they could find
Whistling a tune, though tired and faces lined.

The watchman minding a hole day and night
He kept his brazier burning bright.
As he guarded the road works honestly
He warmed his hands with a mug of tea.

When morning came, he would still be there
Awaiting the relief man to do his share.
Soon the workmen with pickaxes arrive
The money earned helped families survive.

No social benefits of any kind
If they fell out of work, and no more to find
But they would whistle and sing
Working for what a day's work would bring.

The chimney sweep was booked each year
To sweep each chimney free and clear.
With sacks around the fireplace
He pushed his brushes up the chimney space.

Kneeling there with blackened face
He brought the soot down at a cracking pace.
We rushed outside to see his brush
Emerge from the chimney in a rush.

Back inside we told the sweep
Marvelling at the sooty heaps
We had seen the brush waving in the sky
And he heaved it down with a grateful sigh.

Carefully he tied the sacks
And lifted them upon his back.
He spilt no soot throughout the house
As he left as quietly as a mouse.

The kitchen range was the first to be lit.
Laid with paper and then the sticks
Upon which the coal was gently placed
Lit with a match, up the flames raced.

'We've got a good draught,' Mother said with a nod
As she placed her flat iron on the hob.
There were sheets and shirts and everything
That a good day's washing would bring in.

Dad knew the work that was involved
He said, 'I think we've got the problem solved
We'll buy a Wonder washing machine.'
But Mother wasn't really keen.

For a few shillings a week the machine came, soon
Mother discovered the machine was a boon.
The clothes went into a big square tub
No more would Mother at the scrubbing board rub.

The hot water and soap put in with clothes.
A handle was moved to and fro.
When the clothes came out they were clean
As clean as Mother had ever seen.

The mangle still had its job to do
Squeezing out water as the clothes went thru'.
And Mother was very pleased, you see
For now she had time for a cup of tea.

The wireless still worked by accumulators
And Dad did like hearing the football scores
A better reception might be achieved
If we had a radio, Dad believed.

No more accumulators filled with acid
The dangers of this we would be rid.
A radio was finally bought
Our interest immediately caught.

Dad fiddled around with masses of wires
We watched and watched and began to tire.
Dad twiddled knobs, and heard a sound.
More knobs were twisted round and round.

A blast of music filled the room
And we were listening to Jack Payne's tune.
The reception was really very good
And Dad tuned to every station he could.

Many happy hours were spent
Listening to favourite programmes, and content.
Sometimes though the news was bad
On many occasions very sad.

On the radio we heard the newsman say
King George the Fifth has passed away
And as I climbed Croom's Hill that day
I pondered sadly history had changed in every way.

I remembered I had seen the King and Queen.
A very rare occasion it had been.
In Creek Road the crowds had collected
When they heard their Majesties were expected.

They were visiting a building here.
Poor Deptford was drab and austere
Their very presence raised spirits high
And we all cheered as they went by.

Prince Edward would now be King it seemed
But he hadn't married, and had no Queen.
It seemed an American lady was on the scene
And troubles in the Royal Family there had been.

About this time dear Mother was ill.
The doctor said she should live on a hill.
Dad searched around and thought hard and long
For houses were not to be had for a song.

One day he declared he'd found the place
A new estate, on a hill with trees and space.
The air should be fresh as four winds blew
And from this hill there were wonderful views.

We took a bus outside New Cross Station
On the journey we were filled with elation.
Would this place be up to our expectations?
And we chatted about height and elevation

The journey seemed endless, but we must be near.
Past Charlton, the conductor called Woolwich Arsenal here.
We were looking for a very big hill
We'd seen nothing yet to fit the bill.

Around the corners the bus carried on
Then at last the hill we came upon.
The bus chugged up and up so slowly
Round the corner, Plumstead Common we see.

The bus speeded up then stopped at the Globe.
We all got off and crossed the road.
We have a hill yet still to walk
Plum Lane was sheer – we could not talk.

We huffed and puffed our way to the top.
We stayed there, very glad to stop.
A panoramic view we spied for miles
The river, parks and many church spires.

Shrewsbury Park on our left, full of trees
The sun was shining thru' the leaves.
Along the lane we could see them there
Red roofed houses, front doors unpainted and bare.

The showhouse was a real delight
Nicely furnished, it felt just right.
Upstairs there was a room which made us gasp
It contained a wash-hand basin and a bath.

The kitchen held another surprise
An Ideal Boiler from which heat would rise
Hot water from the taps would run.
What a pleasure if we could have one.

The dining room had an open fireplace
The oak surround added even more grace.
The whole room was very bright
French windows let in so much light.

Three bedrooms, two with electric fires
There to give warmth if one desires.
By the bathroom another joy to behold
An inside lavatory worth its weight in gold.

We left the scene, the bus to catch
Dad deep in thought, and Mother to match.
Mesmerised to Deptford home we went.
This was an afternoon well spent.

Dad's face creased with effort of thought.
Could such a house yet be bought?
For it did indeed hold all he sought.
From careful planning it could be wrought.

We all sat down and discussed at length
The pros and cons that all this meant.
And yes a big decision was made
Dad's plans were well and truly laid.

Dad went back to the site next day
For better or worse a deposit to pay.
He picked his spot so carefully sought
On which would rise the house he'd bought.

We had to wait whilst the house was built
But our enthusiasm would never wilt.
We were told it would be ready next year
We bided our time till May was near.

In the meantime a little packing was done
There was work like this for everyone.
Christmas came and went, and May was the date
It seemed very hard to wait and wait

Now older sister was at an age
Where she was able to earn a wage.
She was bright and very earnest
And office work for her was best.

She got her job, and how she loved it
And she helped with expenses just a bit.
Brother too was ready to earn
And his was an office job in a local firm.

On the radio at Christmas time we heard
Prince Edward speak his abdication words.
He had given up the throne to marry his lady
And he left these shores rather gravely.

His brother George took up the reins
With wife Elizabeth he took the strains.
We looked forward to his Coronation
We would have a King for the nation.

So it was in the month of May
Came the long awaited moving day.
The sun was shining as we left our road
Somewhat reluctantly to find our new abode.

We tearfully said goodbye to Auntie Smith.
Between the families there was never a tiff.
A neighbour such as her, would we find again
We would miss her badly, that was plain.

Three went with the moving van
Three to follow and catch a tram.
At Woolwich not a bus to be had
A bus strike was on, for us that was bad.

With groceries and potatoes, bags packed to the brim
For us things were looking very grim.
We walked the bus route to Plumstead Common
As uphill we struggled on and on.

We stopped for breath and asked a passer-by
'In what direction did Plum Lane lie?'
'Straight on until you reach the Globe.'
We took a deep breath and on we strode.

There it was again, and heavily laden
Plum Lane we climbed, what a time it had taken.
We arrived at our chosen home at last.
'Put the kettle on,' Mother gasped.

The furniture was in, and the van had gone
Dad asked us why we had been so long.
He didn't know about the strike
He said, you've all had quite a hike.

The beds were ready, and curtains were up
Tables in place, laid with plate and cup
On Mother's new cooker our first meal was cooked
It was enamelled white, how clean it looked.

And so we were tired, and ready for bed.
We crawled upstairs with feet like lead.
We fell into bed, drooping and yawning
Peacefully sleeping until it was morning.

The weather was perfect, just for us it seemed.
We looked out of the window wherein the sun streamed.
There was the huge garden where Dad laid a lawn.
It seemed we were the luckiest ever born.

Our radio had not yet been fixed
The wires were in a mess and mixed.
The Coronation ceremony we wished to hear
With a radio from next door we heard it loud and clear.

A long wire over the fence was laid.
In the garden we heard history made.
We thanked our neighbour very kindly for this
It really was something we should not miss.

With summer ahead there was a lot to do
Plants for borders and trees one or two
For the lawn an apple and pear.
We hoped a lot of fruit they would bear.

Beyond the lawn vegetables were planned
And ten more fruit trees to fill the land.
Dad made long paths with every care
Planting vegetables, no section left bare.

Mother decided where the washing line should be
Where sheets would flap untangled and free.
The lawn was wide and very long it seemed
Of such expanse and space we had dreamed.

Now paving stones were being put down
White and curving, the road round
At last with greater comfort for our feet
With tarmac down, the estate was clean and neat.

Down the hill Herbert Road lay
Where shopping was done nearly every day.
Like a country village with a variety of shops
We gazed in windows surveying their stock.

Gregs, United Dairies and jewellers there.
So fascinating we would stand and stare
Fishmongers, butchers, woolshops and bakers too
Sweetshops, music and oilshops to name just a few.

It was a quaint place to discover
And we did many trips to help Mother.
With shopping bags we climbed the hill
And we recovered our breath by standing still.

The exercise was good for us
But we often wished we could catch a bus.
And so we got to know the district well.
Upon the family it cast a spell.

Walks in the woods, and the putting green
A golf course, and tennis courts all to be seen.
The water tower standing tall and proud
The noise of rushing water really loud.

This was a heavenly place to live
And we enjoyed all that nature could give
Where squirrels and birds and rabbits were seen
And in the darkness the foxes' eyes gleamed.

Down the hill by the Globe
To Woolwich on a bus we rode
A large market there to enjoy
And traders using every ploy.

We turn the corner to Powis Street
And there before us another treat
With Cuffs and Garretts to explore
And further down the great Co-op store.

Marks and Spencers, and Woolworths to be seen
With Robinson and Taylors our window shopping was keen.
The shops seemed full of lovely things
Like the jewellery shops full of watches and rings.

At these goods we could only look
For to buy we must save the money it took.
In six months maybe we could buy new shoes
Hoping old shoes would last the months through.

But we were happy our parents had achieved
A new home and life for us we believed.
The first winter brought a big snowfall
And we built a snowman six foot tall.

No thoughts of summer holiday this year
With so much countryside so near.
A bus ride, and we were down in Kent.
On these trips we often went.

The garden produced vegetables and fruit
The quality of which was beyond repute.
The months went by with incredible speed
And I wondered if in a job I would succeed.

I joined an agency paying a price
Three shillings and sixpence to be precise.
I waited months and months with hopes held high
At last an interview, and I could but try.

Jobs were few and far between
But what a difference this would mean.
Success was mine, I got the job
At seventeen and sixpence I said, thank God.

This was very good money indeed
And I intended without doubt to succeed
But the first week's wages to the Agency went.
I felt this money was very well spent.

To Southwark by bus and tram each day
I started a good day's work for a good day's pay
Eight thirty through till work was done.
Saturday eight thirty till after one.

Ten shillings for Mum each week we gave
Some for fares and what was left to save.
Dad would ask for a tarpaulin muster
And around the table we would cluster.

We listened to the plan he devised.
If we all subscribed he then advised
A radiogram would have pride of place
In the dining room, there would be space.

A deposit put down, and a payment each week
Our enjoyment now was at its peak.
Programmes received loud and clear
And a few records to play if not too dear.

Begin the Beguine was truly favourite
And again and again we happily played it.
A gentle melody with words to match
With such a song you could relax.

We really had settled and enjoyed our home
We balanced the books without a loan.
Dad hoped in nineteen thirty-nine
We could have a holiday sometime.

In September perhaps it should be
But we would have to wait and see.
Down to Dymchurch we might go
The weather might be our only woe.

The summer was really good and fine
And we waited patiently for holiday time
The newspapers however held disturbing news
As troubles across the Channel grew.

Hitler, head of the German race
Brought worried frowns to Chamberlain's face.
His troops were marching into countries fast
To appease him now was Chamberlain's task.

Dad and Mum remembered World War One
With all its horror, and still with some
The servicemen who had survived
With injured minds, bodies and ruined lives.

Could this happen yet again?
Was this Hitler really insane?
To solve the problems Chamberlain tried
His methods rather meek and mild

To and fro on a plane he'd go
Eventually he would let us know.
'Peace in our Time' he was to declare
As he waved a document in the air.

The British people got on with life.
We'd overcome the trouble and strife.
Peace was ours we all now thought
In plans for war we had not been caught.

The family holiday was now to come
And we could relax in the sun
So down to Dymchurch we six went
The second of September our holiday to commence.

Awakened by the lapping of waves
And church bells practising their octaves
With an Indian summer we were blessed
But the day's events could not be guessed.

September the third, and the news was bad
On radio Chamberlain spoke and was sad
Great Britain was now in a state of war.
We did not realise what was in store.

We walked the beach in balmy air
Thinking thoughts we did not share.
Suddenly the beach was cleared
Whistles blowing, an air raid feared.

Out at sea some objects were seen.
They were in the sky, what could it mean?
Aircraft coming to bomb so soon
And it was barely past noon.

We waited and listened with bated breath.
On the beaches no one was left.
An hour, and whistles blew all clear
No aircraft had been near.

It appears that seagulls approached the shore.
It looked threatening, and even more
With relief we relaxed, and we laughed
To be so shaken by gulls seemed so daft.

So we continued to enjoy our holiday
But what was in our parents' minds, who could say.
Less than twenty years ago they'd fought a war
That had left some minds and hearts so sore.

Home again and back to work routine
From the radio, and papers the news we gleaned
It could be over by Christmas, they said
As the B.E.F. across the Channel sped.

Christmas nineteen thirty-nine drew near.
No peace on the Continent that was clear.
Our gallant soldiers fought long and hard.
At home, for butter, bacon and sugar a ration card.

Chamberlain now ill resigned in May.
Churchill emerged to save the day.
Our survival in his hands now lay.
Eagerly we listened to what he would say.

Our fate in May was far from good
At the end of which alone we stood.
Big ships, small boats of every kind
Anything that floated we had to find.

Our troops pushed back now to the beaches.
With its ugly lessons war teaches.
Roaring aircraft machine-gunned and bombed
Helpless men who for rescue longed.

Mercilessly for days the torture went on
And often men raised their voices in song.
Then the little boats and ships appeared.
Brave men cried and brave men cheered.

Into the water they waded waist high
When rescue boats drifted by.
Willing hands reached out to them
Until the boat was full from stern to stem.

Hearts and minds filled with relief.
No time yet to register grief
For those that died upon the beach
Or those that drowned, help beyond reach.

Screaming Stukas tore through the sky.
On the sands below many would die.
Machine-guns, chattering masters of fate
For those who found no shelter to take.

Boats and ships, some large some small
Stayed at their posts to answer the call.
As dusk fell and anchors weighed
They slide away, and strong men prayed.

Thousands of tired eyes looked for Dover
Trusting and hoping their ordeal was over.
And there it was, home at last
They patiently waited whilst the ships made fast.

Down the gangways they wearily stumbled
With bandaged limbs and heads, no one grumbled.
Home sweet home was never so appreciated
As with hot tea, soup and cigarettes they were greeted.

Through sleepy villages in convoys they went
To resting places where the night was spent
Hospitals were in demand, the need was great.
For news of loved ones families had to wait.

For many families great feelings of relief
But for a large number deeply felt grief.
Stunned perhaps by the immense disaster
The nation wondered if events could get nastier.

Churchill to the nation spoke with passion
His words delivered in heroic fashion
On this island we would fight to defend
In the hills, in the streets whatever Hitler would send

Now Dad around the family table discussed
His thoughts that a shelter was a must.
His weekly pay a fraction too much
He had to buy for safety as such.

He paid the council the required amount
The cost of which he did not count.
His precious lawn was measured with care
At the end of which he planned it there.

He dug a hole that was really deep
Beside the pear tree he wanted to keep.
Partitions put together and bolted tight
Dad said he thought he had it right.

Great mounds of earth placed on the top.
When turfed Dad felt that he could stop.
Satisfied, he laid a wooden floor
Put in the bunks and a wooden door.

A construction like a small porch was added
Double wooden walls with earth were padded
Small oil lamps and torches used for light
If the shelter was needed in the night.

Gas masks had been issued to everyone
In case gas attacks should come.
A decontamination centre was built nearby
That it might be necessary who could deny.

Now as we travelled to work each day
If the sirens went on the bus we'd stay
Watching the aircraft in the sky
Messerschmitts and Hurricanes battling up high.

By Blackwall Tunnel in a traffic jam
Leaning out bus windows the sky to scan.
They were weaving, diving and dodging about
Our brave young pilots were sorting them out.

The German planes were soon dispersed.
On the bus some people cheered and some cursed.
The all-clear sounded and traffic moved on.
From the sky the German planes had gone.

This was quite a frequent event
As the long summer days came and went.
September began with warm and gentle sunshine
We were unaware of the evil it would combine.

One Saturday for the afternoon performance
The Globe was showing a film of some importance
The name of the film was Great Expectations
For my young sister and me a form of education.

Halfway through, the sirens sounded.
Through my head the thought pounded
Should we stay or should we leave?
It might be safer to stay, I believed.

Suddenly gun-fire was heard, and near.
In the cinema we were asked to go to the rear.
The fire exit doors blew open wide
And blue flashes went from side to side

Small pieces of ceiling fell to the floor.
The guns had fired just outside the door.
The horrendous noise an ear-splitting sound
Of gun-fire, and bombs whistling down.

At long last the all-clear was heard.
We left the cinema without a word.
Shaken by this bombing raid, we needed air
But up the hill we would stop and stare.

We were going to have a storm.
The skies were black and it was warm.
We realised then that it was smoke
The seriousness of which Dad spoke.

As the family settled for tea at the table
Keeping as calm as we were able
From the bedrooms we had seen black smoke rising.
'It's the docks,' Dad said, 'which is not surprising.'

'You see, they want to stop supplies,' said Dad
'And from what I've seen it looks bad.'
'They have done a lot of damage there
Today they have certainly had their share.'

And then to our dismay we heard again
The wailing sirens and the engines of planes
The ugly throb of German bombers droning.
In the garden we saw great hordes on the docks homing.

Great black shapes in formation, flying low
Approached the East End to deliver another great blow.
In fading light and with fires still burning bright
They dropped their bombs throughout the night.

A dreadful night of terror and fear
People had lost all they held dear.
Amongst the rubble hurt and dazed
True British grit was amazingly displayed.

The bombers came again and again
By day and night we heard these planes.
The barrage balloon now sited in the park
Was raised and lowered in daylight hours and dark.

Then one Saturday September afternoon
The sirens wailed, the balloon went up none to soon.
A heavy air raid then ensued
During which Dad's shelter's value was proved.

An enormous blast that was very close by
We worried and wondered what had come from the sky.
As the all clear sounded from the shelter we came
And our road would never again be the same.

The road was blown up thirty foot high
House numbered one blown away in the sky
Our doors and windows no longer there
Upstairs floors tilted, and we carefully tested each stair.

The blitz now had really commenced
We heard Lord Haw-Haw's silly comments
It did not deter us nor dim the spirit
We were fighting a war and we would win it.

Hardships yes in many ways
As we battled on through the days
Our food supplies were getting short
Our ships were lost before reaching port.

These merchant sailors without defence kept sailing.
Unsung heroes their courage never failing,
Submarines, mines, and aircraft attacking in the channel,
They sailed on, past sunken ships marked by a funnel.

The tugs went out to meet the ships
With bad weather, and mine infested water came to grips.
They towed the ships with precious cargo back
To be unloaded on to docks burnt and black.

Dad came home a weary man.
We had a temporary address whilst repairs began.
We would soon be back in our own home
But nightly we hear the siren's wailing moan.

From our temporary address along we sped
In single file, which Mum led.
She carried a saucepan full of hot stew
An alarm clock, a torch and knives and forks too.

We carried plates and essentials we needed.
We laughed and giggled, our progress impeded.
Back to Dad's shelter we were bound
For it was there we felt very safe and sound.

Then after Christmas we moved back home
With things around us that were our own.
The nightly raids continued their destruction
Each day we witnessed more devastation.

Railway bridges were targeted too
Left with great holes you could see the sky through
On rails alone, trains traversed the awesome space,
Moving carefully at a very slow pace.

Firemen lost their lives fighting fires
Where flames were licking around church spires.
Hour after hour they battled on
Long after the bombers had gone.

Each day we went to work, our job to do
With a sense of duty to help us through.
Travelling home when darkness had descended
Regular bus and tram service suspended

We climbed on to lorries going our way
Even a pig-transport van often saved the day.
Smelly and dark it was our salvation
It took us nearer our destination.

One March night we had reached Charlton.
In darkness we walked with the usual raid on
My sister and I and a staunch friend
Using what light the searchlights would lend.

We listened to footsteps following behind
And circling great craters that we would find
Suddenly we heard a shout of dismay
So back to the last crater we made our way.

It seemed the footsteps were made by a man.
To fall into the crater was not his plan.
We knelt at the edge of this great hole
To see if we were needed in a rescue role.

"Are you alright?" we shouted down.
"Yes," he replied. "Don't hang around.
Get on your way, and I'll climb out."
This we did with guilt and doubt.

We were by J. Stone when it happened.
Searchlights were making their criss-cross pattern.
A bomber now caught high in the beams
Released a great bomb and down it screamed.

No shelter for us, so we knelt down.
An enormous blast, an enormous sound.
We listened to debris being thrown around.
Eventually we raised ourselves from the ground.

On we went, hoping we might see
Some form of transport, a tram maybe.
We heard a noise some distance away.
A tram approached with its familiar sway.

Its lights were dimmed, but would we be seen?
We hoped the driver's eyesight was keen.
Waving our arms we stood on the line
And to our relief he stopped in time.

We scrambled on with grateful thanks given
But only to Powis Street we were driven.
There we alighted, and ran to the square.
The Gods were with us, a bus was there.

Home again, and the usual routine
To the air raid shelter, not a light to be seen.
Frightening nights of the bomber's moon
We hoped the skies would be cloudy soon.

For ninety-eight nights the bombers came
A mobile gun at night in Plum Lane.
We heard the commanding shout of fire
And we blocked our ears and shut our eyes.

Inside the shelter a light flashed blue,
The gun fired as overhead the bombers flew,
We listened as the engine noises faded
The gun was quiet but we felt jaded.

Then one night in April forty-one
The sirens wailed, more bombers had come
And we heard the monotonous drone overhead
Filling our minds with awesome dread

Our ears filled with a whistling scream
And this was not a horrendous dream.
Four bombs hurtling on their way
We did not have the time to pray.

One and two hit the street below
But three and four dealt us a dreadful blow.
In the vegetable garden number three fell
Number four so close, a noise from hell.

The shelter tipped sideways plunged into darkness
Debris, dirt, dust a swirling choking mess.
An awful silence, and then Dad asked
"Is everybody alright?" he managed to gasp.

One by one we each answered his question
Miraculously no injuries to mention.
"Have a look outside," Dad said to brother.
"The house has gone," he said to Dad and Mother

At break of day brother climbed out again.
That the house was gone that was plain.
He tumbled down a thirty foot hole
Made by the bomb that had taken its toll.

From the shelter we all clambered out.
Everything lost without a doubt.
We had no clothes, no food, nor even money
But alive we were for all to see

To the decontamination station we went
Tired, dirty, and backs slightly bent.
"We thought you were dead," the warden said
As to a hot cup of tea we were led.

Kindly neighbours rallied round
A meal for each at midday was found.
We shall go to Gravesend it was decided.
It was there a very good aunt resided.

Shocked was she when we arrived
And told our story how we'd nearly died
Aunt slept on the floor, her bedroom to share
She gave us her bed, and three slept there.

Her neighbours took the other three
So that they could sleep comfortably.
Exhausted we slept through the night
Awakening next morning to realise our plight

Within a week a house was found to rent.
Into this house we finally went.
We had no furniture, it was completely bare
We used wooden boxes for table and chair.

Borrowed cutlery, plates and spoons
We ate a meal in an empty room.
Dad went out and bought our beds.
At the WVS for blankets we'd had to beg

A zinc bath was another priority
There was no bathroom, but an outside lavatory.
Hot water supply was again a copper.
Mother liked things clean and proper.

So many things we needed and wanted
Like toothbrushes that we had taken for granted.
It was a major problem for the family
But we were alive and surviving gratefully.

Gradually by careful planning and thought
The necessities of life were bought.
It wasn't easy for clothing needed coupons
And even pots and pans were hard to come upon.

The air raids didn't seem quite so frequent
As to and fro to work we went.
Train journeys now were long and hazardous
But the nights in Gravesend peaceful for us.

Dad and brother faced dangers on the river.
Their bags were packed with food by Mother.
She did not know when they would come home
But within the household never a moan.

Little sister resumed her shattered education
In a school lessons were started with dedication.
Prior to this, it was hit and miss to learn
In church halls, spare rooms and huts in turn.

The months of nineteen forty-one passed on
With German bombers looking for targets to bomb.
My first cigarette was smoked in a train
Trapped in a tunnel, it helped take the strain.

In June Hitler's army invaded Russia
It seemed to relieve a lot of pressure.
Slowly in Gravesend the family recovered
Gradually letting go of the trauma suffered.

As Christmas approached the Japs went mad
They bombed Pearl Harbor, the slaughter bad.
Horrific scenes were in the papers.
In the US great demands made on armament makers.

America declared war on Germany and Japan.
It seemed that war the whole world would span.
In our small corner things got quieter
And soon the days were longer and lighter.

Dad thought that to London we could return
And went back home to see what he could learn.
As luck would have it he met a good neighbour
Through the council he could do us a favour

We could rent his house and pay the council.
A family discussion, the usual drill.
Our journeys to work would be less to travel.
Back to an area we loved and knew so well.

So once again we took the chance.
Our few possessions went on in advance
And back to Shooters Hill we went
To another house that was lent to rent.

At Gravesend in school young sister did well
And into grammar school education her marks fell.
The grammar school was Eltham Hill
But to provide the uniform Mother needed skill.

A few clothing coupons each to her we gave.
We were so needy, but knew how to save.
The uniform came into being soon.
A few second-hand things were a boon.

I changed my job about this time
A local one, and success was mine.
A ten minute walk through the park
And arrive for work at eight thirty sharp.

Set in trees, this secret place
Where people worked at quite a pace.
With drawing boards and inventive minds
Expertise created weapon designs.

For they must win, defence is no sin.
When evil prevails the fight begins.
Clocking in, working hard all day
These ordinary people slaved away.

A wonderful spirit filled the people daily
Accepting shortages, and air raids bravely.
Boy friends and husbands away in various forces
Fighting in deserts where the sun scorches.

In the air, and on the seas they battled on
Some in submarines taking watches hours long.
Many were fearful, but it would rarely show.
They fought long and hard with victory slow

Young lads when their country had called them
With shattering times were transformed into men.
Childhood struggles left far behind
The desire to survive filled each mind.

Across the desert sands they fought.
Besides the bullet, disease was caught.
Brains and bodies battled on and on
Until the enemy was beaten and gone.

Great battles fought across the African continent
Montgomery's manoeuvres, and Rommel's forces spent.
British and Allied soldiers had beaten the Hun
Germans and Italians had nowhere to run.

On the Russian front, nineteen forty-three
Russians fought that Stalingrad would be free.
Supreme their efforts in freezing weather
To rid their country of invaders for ever.

They won the battle and turned the tide
Thousands of Russians and Germans died.
Frozen corpses littered the ground
In this climate no mercy is found.

All across the world men fought.
Different races did what they were taught
Some to conquer for evil gain
Oblivious to their victims' pain.

In jungles where a betraying twig would crack
Allied soldiers gallantly fought back.
In prison camps they languished, many died
Of heat, exhaustion, starvation, but some survived.

In concentration camps Jews were murdered
The shivering survivors starved and shuddered
Facing each day, it may be their last
As they watched the smoke from the chimney blast.

The British nation daily battled
Working each day, for victory mattered.
Unaware of the horrors in these heinous places
Time would reveal the evil faces.

The Fire Service decided they wanted me
On a part time basis this was to be.
Kitted out in uniform and tin hat
The names of fire equipment learnt off pat.

One night a week was our stint
We had no time to stop and think.
After a day's work off we went
To Shooters Hill Fire Station where the night was spent.

Between the raids was restless sleep.
A night's sleep was never deep
Air raid sirens so often wailed
Alerting us to danger, it never failed.

The months dragged on with sunshine and rain.
The brave armed forces had their losses and gains.
Cement tank traps across our road were placed
In case the enemy at the corner be faced.

Dad and brother away a lot from home
Towing great structures, their use not known.
Then one sunny June early morning
At breakfast we heard a familiar droning.

Aircraft approaching, an ominous sound.
Out to the garden we went in a bound.
No warning had sounded, we were amazed
As to the sky our eyes were raised.

Bombers and fighters low overhead.
We cheered, not the enemy but ours instead.
Hundreds and hundreds there seemed to be
The noise horrendous, but a joy to see.

A close kept secret about to be known
Rumours about a second front had grown.
It must be, it must be, we hopefully thought
Not knowing of the bloody battles to be fought.

The allies were landing on the French coast.
In hearts and minds it had been no idle boast.
So many men would be lost, or badly injured
And fear of what might happen be endured.

They spilled out from the landing barges
And millions of men went into forward charges.
Footholds were gained for which many paid.
At this high price progress was made.

The weather changed to gales and storms
But nevertheless Mulberry Harbour was formed.
Across stormy waters the structures were towed
On to this construction the necessary supplies flowed.

The allied forces battled for every yard
Every nerve stiffened and on guard
Not knowing where a shell or bullet would land
Willing in their hearts to win a mile as planned.

The quiet French villages were blasted away
The lives of people taken, they had lived their last day
Innocent victims both young and old
And of this, history demands the story be told.

Enemy forces now fully engaged
So it was one day while battles raged
A mysterious explosion was heard in London.
It was loud and clearly a massive one.

We thought a gasometer it must be
But people had watched the sky to see
A plane on fire, the engine roaring
The ominous thud, and debris soaring.

There were many rumours bandied about
But very soon the truth was out.
Hitler had launched a flying bomb
No pilot, but something we had to shelter from.

Soon they came thick and fast
Our Spitfire pilots chasing and flying past
Trying to catch them and tip their wings.
We watched their bravery with these inhuman things.

In our park we looked out over Kent
Barrage balloons stationed across the sky went.
We watched these fiendish flying bombs
Break through the defence, flying on and on.

Racing back to our Anderson shelter
We tumbled in helter skelter
Listening for the engines to stop
And the silence when they began to drop

The hissing air as they began to crash.
Into innocent abodes they would smash
Death and destruction all around
When these mechanical bombs hit the ground.

Once again people balanced their lives
Determined against all odds to survive.
Daily work continued on and at night
The civilians would not give up the fight.

At our place of work the V One was tracked
Each one had its journey carefully mapped.
One of these found us as it came in low
Its speed of flight beginning to slow.

Its wing caught on a roof top wall.
Behind the building we watched it fall.
Luck was in, it was open ground.
It blew two wooden buildings away, we found.

Walking home to midday lunch another day
My sister and I went the Dot Lane way.
Beside the park it was an unmade road
With deep holes filled where springs rose.

The birds were singing, but what we heard
Was a sinister sound, not a bird
The hissing noise, we now knew well
This was close, from the sound we could tell.

Above the bushes just ahead we saw
The V One's hideous body, with the explosives it bore.
We dropped to ground, heads covered with hands
Fearful of where the thing would land.

Luck was with us, on the side of the hill
The ground dropped away and the damage nil
For it fell in allotments, the earth blown high.
We rose from the ground to see a crater nearby.

We looked at each other and burst into laughter
Quickly followed by consternation after.
Covered in muddy water head to foot
It looked as though we had fallen into soot.

Our wardrobes were sparse, that was the problem
It was always a question of wash and wear them.
We changed our clothes, and again felt clean
It wasn't as bad as it might have been.

Sunny days since June when the first V One came
Sirens wailed, and nights in shelters again.
September came and the nights were longer
Then came a louder bang on which to ponder.

Hitler had sent a monster through the sky
Making sure that many more civilians would die.
The V Two rocket bomb, his latest weapon
Houses and schools vanished in a second.

Grief amongst the British was great
We had lost so many people of late.
Our forces still were fighting hard
Battling on yard by yard.

The news from the east never seemed good
But the tide was turning as we hoped it would.
The forgotten army, they called these men
And so it seemed to so many of them.

Back home again we faced sudden horror
With these V Twos would there be a tomorrow?
Would we be here in the next minute or two?
Would we live the next hour through?

Facing these terrors one thought it through
There was so much danger, that was true.
If one walked to the corner and still alive
It was then possible one would survive.

So fear was put aside to some extent.
It was live or die, that's what it meant.
No need to rush to the shelter again
We lived our lives and accepted the strain.

My sister and I now slept in bed at night
To avoid the cockroaches and beetles that bite
The comfort for us was so supreme
In the morning we woke feeling rested and clean.

A hole in the roof and rain dripping through
It dropped on our faces but made us laugh too.
So little to pay for a good night's rest
And we faced each day with a little more zest

We thought we were slim, but in reality thin.
Rations were sparse, with powdered egg from a tin
Powdered potatoes, and something called Spam.
For years we had not seen a slice of real ham.

Dad bought a few chicks he nurtured with care
Then one day the first fresh egg was there.
We voted that Dad should enjoy this treat
And it was with pleasure we watched him eat.

Soon the hens were laying well
A nourishing meal in a golden shell.
They each had a name, and when called they came
Each one had a character, and became very tame.

They were our pets and we loved them all
Strutting the garden proud and tall
With any eggs that we had to spare
Our neighbours were given each a share.

This brightened the day with food so short
To tighten our belts we had been taught
Things were a bit better now we had hens
Mother could make a cake now and then

The evil V Two bombs thru' the air still tore
In the late months of nineteen forty-four.
Nearly five years of struggle in a ghastly war
We longed for peace more and more.

Christmas approached and people were tired
But with grit and determination they were fired.
Having taken so much, we were giving it back
The allies were on a winning track

I remember that Christmas I was twenty-one
To celebrate with a glass of wine was fun.
No party, as rations were exceptionally low
What the New Year would bring we did not know

The nights again were long, and daylight so short
But maybe things were more hopeful we thought.
Battles raging on the Continent were being won
We had got Hitler's armies on the run.

February weather icy cold and wet
Russian eyes upon Berlin were set.
On maps the battle lines were drawn
From bitter struggles new hope was born.

The German forces were now being squeezed
As cities and towns were being freed.
V Ones and V Twos battered South-East England still.
Hitler was still trying to impose his evil will.

Daily, civilians were killed or maimed
But morale and courage were maintained
People smiled and joked with each other
Our real emotions we tried to smother.

Churchill, seeking to ease our burdensome needs
Made sure the V-weapon sites were found with speed.
By March 27 the V Twos ceased
And daily life was immensely eased.

We really felt that life had improved
As the battles closer to Berlin had moved
Now the Germans were struggling hard
And every escape for them was barred.

As the allies progressed, our hearts were lifted
And every piece of news was sifted
Amongst which were horrors beyond belief
As the armies brought the concentration camps relief.

People looking like walking bones
Crept out uttering wailing moans
Watching soldiers hardened by war
Stood aghast at what they saw

Rescue had come, for some too late
The world learned of their hideous fate.
The scenes were filmed that we should know
And into these areas aid would flow.

Our own sufferings faded fast
As the armies took on this awesome task.
Doctors, nurses, medication were drafted in.
Long recuperation could now begin.

Many more camps were now found
As the allies captured more ground.
Again and again gruesome sights were seen
These suffering victims in a living hell had been.

April brought us better news
Hitler had no remedy to choose.
The evil that he himself had released
Was returning to defeat the beast.

At the river Elbe the armies met
For the Americans and Russians a long hard trek.
An arm was raised in a friendly wave
Then shouts and cheers each army gave.

Hitler now confused and mad
Yet realised his position was bad.
He married Eva Braun, his devoted friend
But did she know her life would end?

Mussolini and mistress on April 25 fled
No doubt filled with fear and dread.
They were caught and then shot dead.
The lurid details in the newspapers we read.

The Italian nation seemed not dismayed
No longer believing in the role he played.
They were glad an evil tyrant had gone
He led them into war, and he was wrong.

Meanwhile the Russians advanced upon Berlin.
The fighting there was immensely grim.
Hitler in his bunker had hidden
With Eva and his faithful dog at his bidding.

The last day of April and nowhere to run
Hitler produced poison and gun
His dog lay dead, and a shot was heard
And soon the world would hear the word

Hitler was dead, removed from the scene.
The conflict might end, it would seem
But a stubborn race does not easily give in
Even though the situation is grim.

Here in Britain we waited tensely
Our spirits and hopes lifted immensely.
Then on the fourth of May the first German surrendered.
It seemed at last hostilities had ended.

On all fronts on May the seventh
There were long awaited historical events.
Unconditional surrender was achieved.
Now we could relax, it was believed.

With a day off from work on the eighth
With our country we had kept faith.
We listened enraptured to Churchill's voice
And we had every reason to rejoice.

We had tuned in the radio and awaited his words
His speech the sweetest we had ever heard.
For us in the South East enormous relief
Amidst the joy, and amidst the grief.

So many had given their all, their lives
The evidence of their courage still survives.
At the Palace thousands of people congregated
For the King and Queen the masses waited.

On the balcony with Churchill they stood.
The people cheered as long as they could.
Immeasurable joy expressed in a roar
As the people cheered and sang even more.

In Trafalgar Square the scene repeated.
Long years of suffering now completed
Time for street parties to celebrate.
Happy children everywhere could hardly wait.

From larders precious rations were donated
Cakes, jellies made, the day awaited.
The sun shone and trestle tables laid
The party began, the memory never to fade.

Truly the war in Europe had ceased
But war was still raging in the Far East
Allied soldiers fighting in jungle heat
Sweating and suffering, never thinking of defeat.

Military minds continued to plan
To outmanoeuvre a warring Japan.
The suffering of prisoners, the extent unknown
Only later revealed when films were shown.

Starving, ill prisoners slaved each day
Forced by the Japanese to build a railway.
Beaten by guards when stopping to rest
To stay alive it tested the best.

The horrors of this Far East war
Continued for a few months more.
Then we heard of the atomic bomb
The end of the war would not be long.

The horrendous bomb would end the war
Save allied lives faster than before.
Many people pondered its use
For it would let all hell loose.

A plane took off with its hideous cargo
To be dropped on Japan, far below
Hiroshima's innocent people had started their day
But in one mightiest flash in ashes they lay.

A mushroom cloud rose high in the sky
Seen by the plane crew as they flew by.
Stunned, somewhat silent, they returned to base.
A new type of warfare the world now had to face.

August the sixth, nineteen forty-five
Was the day that Hiroshima died.
The Japanese nation would not bend
Taking whatever the allies may send.

August the ninth of the same year
Nagasaki had much to fear.
A plane approached with another bomb.
Seconds later Nagasaki had gone.

Those that survived were terribly injured
Horrific burns to be long endured.
At last the Emperor decided to act
His nation could take no more in fact.

On the fifteenth V.J. Day was declared.
A feeling of relief world wide was shared.
The Allies' surrender treaty had been agreed
No more mortal combat would we need.

Again thousands gathered in Trafalgar Square.
This time Mother and I were there.
We could almost touch the joys of the throngs
We really could forget the bombs.

It was over, all over, all over
And men returned, their first sight of England, Dover
The world would be a better place, we thought
For this so many had given their lives and fought.

And food and clothing would be in the shops
As much as you needed of meat or chops
Vegetables galore with lots of choice
Such abundance of food we could rejoice.

In reality all commodities were short
Rationing continued of necessary things bought.
But our hearts and minds were free of fear
And our lives would be better year by year.

Houses, factories, buildings lost in war
Would be rebuilt more or less as before.
Plans to improve all areas were made
To heal the scars and help bad memories fade.

So that was life as I remember
Years twenty-three to forty-five in number.
We all looked forward to a better life
After all the years of suffering and strife.